Contents

SPORTS METAPHORS 4

Cricket 101 and Metaphors...4

Baseball vs Cricket 5

Bowled Out...5

Yorker 6

Bowl a Googly 6

Sticky Wicket 6

Hit for Six 7

It's Just Not Cricket 7

A Good Innings 8

Second Innings 8

On Back Foot...9

Boxing 101 and Metaphors...10

Boxing Metaphors in News Headlines 10

Boxing Metaphors in Tablet Wars..11

Examples of Boxing Metaphors in Everyday Use....................11

Boxing Day..12

Boxing metaphors in Politics..12

Football 101 and Metaphors 13

Football Metaphors in Politics..13

A Work Conversation Sprinkled with Football Metaphors......14

Football 101 14

Football Traditions 15

Controversial Aspects of Football 15

Baseball 101 and Metaphors...16

Seventh Inning Stretch..16

Baseball Metaphors and Idioms 17

Hit the Ball out of the Park 17

Pinch Hitter 17

Touch Base 17

RELIGIOUS METAPHORS 19

Expressions with Religious Origins – Devil.....................................19

The Devil 19

Between the Devil and the Deep Blue Sea 20

Better the Devil you know 21

Devil-may-care 21

Daredevil 22

Making a Deal with the Devil...22

Devil's Advocate 23

The Devil is in the Details 24

The Horn Effect 25

Devil Food, Devil Sports and Devil Clothes 25

Expressions with Religious Origins -Angels and Heaven...........26

Angels...26

Heaven 29

Expressions with Religious Origins -God 33

God 33

Taking God's Name in Vain 34

As God is my Witness 35

Act of God - Force Majeure 36

Alpha and Omega 36

Fit for the Gods...37

Nectar of the Gods..37

Greek God...38

God's country..38

Godspeed 39

The Hand of God 40

God of Cricket 41

God's Gift to Mankind 42

Godforsaken...42

Man Proposes, God Disposes 43

God Helps Those Who Help Themselves....................44

God Works in Mysterious Ways 45

Put the Fear of God into Someone.............................45

And God said Let there be Light and there was Light.............46

Cleanliness is next to Godliness 47

SPORTS METAPHORS

Cricket 101 and Metaphors

I grew up on a diet of cricket in India, and media in cricket-loving countries use cricket related metaphors all around. When I immigrated to the US, I was unable to relate to baseball metaphors until I had lived here a few years. It was easier for me to understand baseball when the similarities and differences with cricket were pointed out. Throughout this blog post, I will compare the two sports, but will also focus on the metaphors used in cricket.

Baseball vs Cricket

Both are bat and ball games. In both games, there are two teams: one batting and the other bowling. The team batting attempts to score runs by hitting the ball with the bat, while the team bowling attempts to reduce the runs and get the players out.

In cricket, there are three wooden wickets or stumps that support two horizontal bails behind the batsman. The batsman always guards those stumps by his person or bat.

In baseball, a batter defends the invisible strike zone. Think of an imaginary rectangle roughly between the knees and shoulders of the batter over the home plate.

Bowling in baseball is full-toss and the ball comes straight at the batter. In cricket, the ball usually bounces once prior to reaching the batsman.

A pitch in cricket is the distance between the two sets of wickets. A pitch in baseball is delivery of the ball.

If a pitched ball passes inside the strike zone without the batter hitting it or if the batter swings and misses the ball , that's a strike. A batter strikes out after three strikes. Striking out in baseball is like being bowled out in cricket.

Bowled Out

One of the ways a batsman gets out in cricket is if one of the bails is dislodged by a ball. A batsman can be **"bowled out"** or **"clean bowled"**. In both cases the ball strikes down at least one of the bails. However, when a batsman gets out by a ball that strikes down a bail without touching the batsman's person or bat, the batsman is called as having been **"clean bowled"**. While the phrase "bowled out" represents that you are out of the game or beaten on the issue at hand; clean bowled" is metaphorically used to represent that a person has been completely taken over. Here are some examples on usage from media headlines:

*"When Pak media **bowled out** Imran Khan for his comments on Narendra Modi"*

*"Not a single car sold? Auto makers in India may be **bowled out** for duck in April"*

*"Yorkshire cricketer **bowled out** by £140k tax bill"*

*"Indian Prime Minister has <u>clean-bowled</u> Pakistan's prime minister with Kashmir **yorker**" (Note that Kashmir is a disputed border state)*

"Netizens <u>clean-bowled</u> by a heart touching video of a mother-son duo playing cricket"

Yorker

A "**yorker**" is a ball in cricket that hits the pitch around the feet of the batsman, making it difficult for the batsman to defend the wickets with a normal batting stance. More often than out, a yorker results in the ball striking the wickets. There are many theories around it's origin. One such theory points the origin to a phrase used in the eighteenth century "to come Yorkshire" or "to put a Yorkshire" on someone, meaning to cheat or dupe them.

Bowl a Googly

A **googly** is a deceptive delivery, where the ball spins after pitching and goes in a different direction than where the batsman was expecting to hit. Metaphorically, to "**bowl a googly**" means to do something unexpected.

"Boris Johnson <u>bowled a googly</u> to thousands of cricketers across the country today when he said the sport could not be allowed to restart"

"In the game of words, Kerala police <u>bowl a googly</u>" (Kerala is a state in India)

Google did not get its name from the same source of googly; it was mis spelled from the word googol. The origin of googly is a little unclear, some theories point to a combination of "goo" and "guile" and some point to "google eyes".

Sticky Wicket

When the area around the wicket is sticky or damp due to recent rain, the ball does not tend to bounce well. A sticky wicket represents a difficult circumstance, as seen below.

"Indian expats with expired visas on <u>sticky wicket</u>"

"Natural rubber sector on a <u>sticky wicket</u>

Hit for Six

While a batter scores a run in baseball by running and completing a round of the four bases, run scoring in cricket is a little different.

A cricket batsman can score a single, double or three runs by hitting the ball and running between the two sets of wickets. Four runs are scored if the batsman hits the ball, and it bounces or touches the ground at least once prior to hitting the boundary. Unlike baseball, there is no foul territory in cricket and the batsman can hit the ball anywhere. This is assuming that a fielder does not dislodge a wicket before either of the two batsmen have reached their respective creases or the ball is not caught by a fielder (like a fly-out in baseball)

If the batsman hits the ball over the boundary, it is six runs; the maximum runs for one cricket shot. If the bowler is hit for a six by the batsman, it is a blow to the bowler. Similar usage below highlights the emotional or physical impact of being "hit for six".

"Cricket is hit for six as coronavirus pandemic leaves county clubs with cash black hole"

"Hit for six by a devastating stroke, this author played on and got his book finished"

It's Just Not Cricket

Cricket has traditionally been called **a gentleman's game**, although some claim that is a victorian notion and not applicable today. When you hear the phrase "It's not cricket", it refers to unjust or unsportsmanlike behavior, as was exemplified in the cricket ball tampering incident in 2018.

"It's just not cricket: Fans hit for six at the ticket office"

"It's just not cricket: Harbhajan urges fans not to get caught out by COVID-19" - Harbhajan is a popular cricketer in India.

"Why These Indians and Pakistanis Rarely Discuss Tensions: It's Just Not Cricket"

For context, Pakistan was once a part of India. When the British agreed to give India it's independence in 1947, they split off Pakistan into a separate country. There have been constant border disputes between the two countries.

A Good Innings

Another popular phrase that comes from cricket is regarding "**a good innings**". In cricket, "**innings**" is used for both a single innings and for multiple ones.

Let us first understand **innings** in cricket. There are basically two types of cricket formats played internationally: limited overs (one-day internationals and Twenty20) and test cricket. In the limited overs matches, there are two innings where each team gets one turn to bat and a certain number of overs per inning (one over is six balls). In test cricket, there are usually two innings per team and no limit on the number of overs per inning. This means that each team gets to bowl and bat twice.

Technically, a team in test cricket can have a long first inning until all their batsmen have been bowled out. However, often, the captain of the team declares an inning if he or she feels that the team has scored sufficient runs. To win in test cricket, a team must bowl out all batsmen from the opposing team in at least two innings and score more runs, so the other innings must happen or else the match will be considered a draw.

If a team has set a high target number of runs in their inning, then they have **a good innings**. Or if an individual batsman has scored a good number of runs, then they are considered to have had **a good innings**. Unlike baseball, a batsman can bat in cricket until they are out.

In the metaphorical context, "**a good innings**" refers to when someone has had a good run at life or in their career. See examples below:

"Decade's medical advances may expand our notion of <u>a good innings</u> "

"World War Two veteran, dies at 103 after <u>a good innings</u> "

Second Innings

A **second innings** usually refers to retirement or a comeback or a second career.

The headline of a news article on a popular Bollywood actor is

"Saif Ali Khan on his <u>second innings</u> in Bollywood. The actor was not seen on the silver screen for a long time before making a banging comeback"

Another headline on a state in India gives an example. For context, MBBS is the term for an undergraduate medical degree in India.

*"**Second innings**: 64-year-old retired bank official in Odisha enrolls in MBBS"*

On Back Foot

To be **on the back foot** means to be put in a defensive position, to be in retreat, to be knocked off balance.

It is derived from cricket when the player puts all the weight on the back foot in the face of a short ball and plays it safely. Going forward to hit the ball may increase the batsman's chances of getting out. Going back into the crease and hitting the ball at the top of its bounce is a safe and defensive stance.

An equivalent boxing metaphor is to be on the ropes which you can read about in the chapter on boxing metaphors.

"Gold <u>on back foot</u> as investors flock to safety of dollar"

"Hong Kong seethes 1 year on, but protesters <u>on back foot</u> "

"Social networks <u>on back foot</u> as digital campaigns expand tactics"

Dear Reader, Hollywood actor Robin Williams' perspective was that *"Cricket is basically baseball on valium"*; would you choose to agree or disagree?

As you ponder over this, I end with lines from an article which reviews a popular Bollywood movie and uses several metaphors from cricket:

*"The disputed house at the center of the film's plot is called 'Second Innings House': the old men living in it determined to play their '<u>second innings</u>' in life on the 'front-foot', after having played the 'first innings on the **back-foot**'. When Gandhi asks the protagonist to follow the path of truth, he responds by articulating his doubts in the language of cricket. The truth would get him '**clean-bowled**'.*

Boxing 101 and Metaphors

Boxing has come a long way in America, from its golden days of legends as Muhammad Ali and Evander Holyfield in the second half of the 19th century. The 20th century has seen much of its glory snatched away by Mixed Martial Arts (MMA). However, one thing has not changed and that is the wide usage of Boxing metaphors and catch phrases in everyday language.

Boxing Metaphors in News Headlines

A quick scan of recent news headlines shows that boxing metaphors are used in reporting of business, politics, trade ... pretty much everywhere.

> *"China Will Dominate High-Tech Unless the United States Takes Off the Gloves "*

> *"It's a knockout: how the English language is rife with boxing metaphors"*

> *"Amazon, Facebook, and Google come out swinging after being slammed with an 'unjustifiable' new tax on their sales "*

Boxing Metaphors in Tablet Wars

Another great example is below, where I quote from a <u>***blogpost***</u> discussing tablet wars.

"The tablet wars just got tougher. Before, Apple was ***duking it out*** with Samsung, and Amazon but now there's a new ***contender for the crown*** of best tablet. Google have ***entered the ring*** with the Nexus 7. Apple used to be the ***undisputed heavyweight tablet champion*** but then came along Samsung who became a serious contender. Yes, Apple created the whole market and is incredibly popular due to quality of product but Samsung now sell more tablets some say. Google are now ***going head to head*** with Apple to become the number 1 tablet producer. Their tablet may be smaller but is a lot cheaper. Both companies are now ***trading punches*** in the advertising war. The web is full of comparisons saying which is best and why. It seems like nobody is ***holding any punches.*** Sales and orders of the Nexus are so big that Google can't deal with them. People are even calling the Nexus the iPad killer, saying that the Nexus is a real ***knock out.*** It looks great and is very comfortable to hold. Make no mistake, ***the gloves are off*** and both companies are ***coming out fighting.*** With big companies like these seeking world domination they ***take no prisoners.*** At the moment it seems like ***round 1 goes to*** the Nexus but Apple isn't ready to ***throw the towel in*** just yet. Rumours are that an iPad is about to ***throw the next punch*** as the iPad mini will be launched soon. It looks like Apple are ***not out for the count*** yet.

And check this <u>**one**</u> from a blogpost that discusses how rife the English language is with Boxing Metaphors.

Examples of Boxing Metaphors in Everyday Use

*"We like to say that we will **come out swinging, pack a punch** and, hopefully, **beat our opponent to the punch.** But we must remember to play fair and not **hit below the belt** – a low blow is unsportsmanlike. There is a time to **pull our punches** and a time to let loose; give an honest opinion, even if it upsets or offends. And when **the gloves are off**, no restraint or mercy is shown. By stunning our opponent with a blow for a 10-count, we hope to win by a*

> *knockout. In adverse circumstances, we **roll with the punches** to adapt, and aim not to end up **on the ropes**, near collapse or defeat. If we can't stand up after a hard blow, we are **down or out for the count**."*

Like me, you may be mistaken into thinking that the metaphor "**come out swinging**" originated from baseball. But it has its origins from *boxing*. Of course, I didn't have a clue why "**to duke it out**" referred to putting up your fists and preparing from a fight until I read the *history and origin* of the phrase. A vulnerability referred to as a "*glass jaw*" made sense once I realized that a boxer' limited ability to absorb blows on the chin made them a soft target for knockout blows.

Boxing Day

One thing that is not celebrated in the US is *Boxing Day,* which refers to the day after Christmas . This is celebrated in most current and former English colonies such as Canada, Australia, and Great Britain. This holiday does not have anything to do with the pugilistic sport of boxing; however, it was traditionally celebrated when servants received "boxed" gifts from their masters. It has now been commercialized and turned into one of the busiest shopping days in those countries like Thanksgiving.

Boxing metaphors in Politics

Other boxing metaphors commonly used in politics, such as "**rope-a-dope**", "**on the ropes**", "**slug it out**" will be covered in another eBook on Political metaphors.

Football 101 and Metaphors

While **_baseball may be America's favorite pastime_**, I quickly discovered that Football is called America's passion for a reason. This blog post attempts to introduce some basic 101 Football concepts and metaphors related to Football that I have encountered in my social and work life.

Football Metaphors in Politics

Politicians such as **_Condoleezza Rice and Dick Cheney have encountered language barriers when_** they have used Football's metaphors to describe political events to other countries. Football has been used in political campaigns such as when **_Obama attacked Romney_**. Sensitive issues such as healthcare , **_nuclear energy_** and abortion might seem to become **_political football_** at times when they become partisan.

A Work Conversation Sprinkled with Football Metaphors

Although a bit exaggerated, the following fictional example of a work-related conversation with a sprinkling of football metaphors gives a great example of how common the usage is in daily life.

> *"The project team is good at **basic blocking and tackling** but rather than be an <u>armchair quarterback</u>, I'm going to <u>run interference</u> in all the working sessions of the project to make sure the team stays on track. I might do <u>end arounds</u> bureaucratic procedures. I just hope the team won't be <u>stopped at the one-yard line</u> as what happened in the last project. <u>Going on a blitz</u> in the last two weeks to **push the project over the goal** seems like an acceptable option."*

> *"Hey, can you help me find resources for this project that I'm getting ready to <u>kickoff</u>? Please do not <u>punt</u> and redirect me to Jane Doe. This is a very important project for me, and I've been asked to <u>carry the ball</u>. We have a general <u>game plan</u> but no solid <u>playbook</u> for implementation. On top of that, I feel like my sponsors are constantly <u>moving the goalposts</u>. I really don't want to <u>fumble</u> this project and <u>drop the ball</u> . I've got to <u>tackle the situation</u> else I'm going to be <u>sidelined</u> in this company."*

> *"If I have to make a <u>hail mary</u> effort to push this project through when it's in the **red zone**, I am going to do it. Because if we fail, then all the <u>Monday morning quarterbacks</u> in office will be giving me advice on how I could have done a better job managing the project."*

The above examples bring home how embedded sports jargon is in popular speech. As a new immigrant in this country, I would have <u>*a deer in headlights look*</u> when exposed to these cliches , idioms and jargon. Of course, I had heard of football, but it was what America calls soccer and most other countries call football.

Football 101

At first, I was curious about the <u>*origins of American football*</u> and wanted to know if it was a form of rugby. As I watched my first super bowl , primarily for the commercials, there were many terms that I didn't understand - <u>*fumble*</u>, <u>*intercept*</u>, <u>*sack*</u>, <u>*line of scrimmage*</u>, **the snap** and **safety** to name a few. Once I figured out that each team had to move the ball 10 yards in **four downs** to continue to retain possession of it, things got clearer.

The next super bowl was not as difficult to comprehend. By then I had gathered that each team's quarterback is kind of like the general. There were *two teams with 11 players* each on the field. A <u>touchdown was worth 6 points</u> and a field goal was 3 points. Understanding the *different football positions* such as Wide Receivers, Running Back, Linebacker, Cornerback took me a few more years.

Football Traditions

I've come a long way since those early years when I didn't understand the NFL draft or the concept of playoffs. I've come to appreciate American football traditions such as *wearing eye black*, **tailgating** and *watching football on Thanksgiving*. I have not joined a fantasy football league yet, though.

Controversial Aspects of Football

Media coverage on controversial aspects of football such as ***Colin Kaepernick kneeling during the national anthem*** have intrigued me. Concussions and their impact on the mental health of football players still shakes me. I am thankful that children now have the option of playing flag football along with tackle football.

Hopefully, my introduction to the *gridiron game* will help others come up to speed faster than it did for me when I was new to the sport and this country.

Baseball 101 and Metaphors

Over the years, it has become apparent to me that Baseball holds a unique place in America's soul. So much so that the **_ceremonial first pitch_** to mark the opening season of baseball is often thrown by a US President.

I grew up in India on a staple diet of cricket, and baseball seemed very unfamiliar to me at first. But learning about the similarities and differences with cricket helped.

Seventh Inning Stretch

The first time I attended a baseball game, I was puzzled by the **_seventh inning stretch_**. The crowd got to their feet and started singing an unfamiliar song.

My friend told me that this tradition usually takes place in between the two halves of the seventh inning and is an opportunity for the players and the audience to take a break, stretch their legs and eat a snack. The crowd usually sings to the song _**Take Me Out to the Ball Game**_. True to the chorus, which talks about peanuts and crackerjack, they are some of the staples always offered at a baseball game, along with other food such as hot dogs, nachos and soda.

Baseball Metaphors and Idioms

My introduction to Baseball metaphors occurred early on when I was told by my manager to _**hit the ball out of the park**_ when working on a marquee customer's project. I started looking out of the windows for the park and wondering where the ball was.

To save others from similar embarrassment, below are examples of commonly used metaphors from the national sport of America.

Hit the Ball out of the Park

To hit the ball out of the park means to do something exceedingly well or to do a stellar job. It is also sometimes expressed as **knock it out of the park**. Baseball is a bat and ball game with two opposing teams. The team that wins is the one that scores the most runs. The venue where baseball is played is shaped like a diamond and is called the ballpark. _To hit the ball out of the park_ means to hit a home run which lands outside of the ballpark flying over all the spectator's seats and landing outside the stadium.

Pinch Hitter

Another metaphor that originates from baseball is _pinch hitter_. In baseball, a pinch hitter is a batter used as a substitute for another batter, usually at a critical point.

Touch Base

How about being asked to _**touch base**_ with a colleague at work to put a _**ballpark estimate**_ together for an upcoming project? Baseball has a 'Home Plate' and three 'Bases' (First base, Second base, Third base). Together, the bases form a diamond shape. The batter receives the pitch at the home plate and needs to touch 1st base, 2nd base and third base in sequence before returning to the home plate. The batter is then rewarded with a run.

Based on the above, the most common interpretation of touching base is to check in. There are other theories around the origin of this phrase, the most interesting one being the military one, where military units on a mission frequently connect with their base.

Ballpark estimate and **ballpark figure** mean the same - an approximation. The phrase **your estimate is in the ballpark** means that the estimate is in range. The phrase seems to have originated from the time when the commentator of a baseball game would estimate the size of the audience by looking around.

We are not done yet. As famous baseball player Yogi Berra would say "It ain't over till it's over."

> *"I do hope I'm **batting a thousand** with my posts. You may think I'm trying to enter into the **big leagues**, but for now I'll take a **rain check** on those. I am really not trying to **play hardball**, just trying to write well for my readers and **cover all my bases** so I can **hit a home run** and it's not a **hit or miss** situation. Life does sometimes **throw a curve ball** or things will **come out of left field** and **catch me off base** and I'll give up writing before I **reach first base**. But I really need to **step up to the plate** and **swing for the fences** even though some of the things I am writing about aren't really **in my wheelhouse** before a **whole new ballgame** begins."*

RELIGIOUS METAPHORS

Expressions with Religious Origins – Devil

In the movie The Italian Job, John Bridger quips:

"Trust everyone, just don't trust the *devil inside them*."

Am I the only one who has wondered why the *devil hides in the details* or why facing the deep blue sea is considered as difficult a choice as facing the devil? There are many common figures of speech that have religious connotations.

But first, a disclaimer. Religion is complicated and there can be different versions of stories and beliefs. The intention of this blog post is not to hurt anyone's sentiments or feelings.

The Devil

We will start off by looking at figures of speech where the devil figures prominently. *"Handsome devil"*, *"The devil incarnate"*, *"Poor devil"*, *"What in the devil* do you make of this", *"What the devil's* gotten into you?" are all used in everyday language.

While the devil is mostly used in the noun form, it can also be used as a verb. *To Bedevil* is to be a little bit like the devil and to cause trouble, distress or annoyance, ***bedeviled*** is the adjective. Devilling is a legal term in some countries (UK, Australia). Per this source, ***devilling*** is a practice among self-employed barristers by which one barrister obtains the assistance of another, usually, amore junior, barrister to carry out work to help the first barrister discharge his instructions.

The classic definition of the devil however, per Wikipedia, is "In mainstream Christianity, the **Devil** (or Satan) is a fallen angel who rebelled against God. A fallen angel is one who was expelled from heaven."

Between the Devil and the Deep Blue Sea

A rarely known meaning of the devil is used to refer to the seam on a wooden ship's hull. To keep this seam caulked, a sailor would have had to stand on the edge of the deck, and the sailor would have been between the devil (seam) and the deep sea. And so, there are divided opinions on whether the origin of the phrase ***Between the devil and the deep blue sea*** is nautical or religious. If religious, then the phrase could also refer to a difficult choice between drowning (deep blue sea) and damnation (the devil).

Whatever the origin, the phrase means to be caught in a dilemma between two equally difficult choices. As the following headlines illustrate,

"Afghan Refugees Caught Between Devil and Deep Blue Sea"

"Journalists in Balochistan: Caught Between the Devil and Deep Blue Sea".

Another figure of speech that conveys similar meaning is ***Between a rock and a hard place***. The phrase ***Damned if you do damned if you don't*** is slightly different. Per the latter phrase, the person in the specific situation will be blamed no matter what choice they take.

Better the Devil you know

Out of two choices, if you are somewhat familiar with one of them, then it is ***Better the devil you know than the one you don't***. This proverb is sometimes used in its shortened version ***Better the devil you know*** as in the following headline,

"*<u>Better the devil you know</u>: the inside story of how Judith Collins became National's leader*"

The full version of the phrase appears in this <u>Bloomberg news article</u> discussing rich Americans moving money,

"*Not every adviser agrees that it's necessary to pay extra in 2020 to avoid hypothetical tax hikes in the future, because deferring taxes still has financial advantages. But for some clients,* "***The devil you know is better than the devil you don't know***".

Unsurprisingly, the devil appears as the representation of evil in most figures of speech. However, there is nothing sinister when the object of a discussion unexpectedly appears on the scene as in the phrase ***Speak of the devil and he shall appear***. It is simply an issue of timing. This interesting <u>blog post</u> has an equivalent phrase from every well-known language in the world.

When you ***give the devil his due***, you are simply acknowledging the good even in a person you may dislike. This phrase also occurs in the classic novel "*Don Quixote*" by Miguel Cervantes.

Devil-may-care

I guess being a ***daredevil*** or having a ***devil-may-care*** attitude is better than being in ***league with the devil***, ***selling your soul to the devil*** or making a ***deal with the devil***. Per <u>this source</u>, the origin of **devil-may-care** probably dates back to the seventeenth century during the Golden Age of Piracy when pirates were recklessly carefree and unconcerned with consequences of their piracy. The devil would still care about their actions and thus the expression came into being, which in its fuller form is ***The devil-may-care, but***

I do not. Even the royals and quarterbacks are not spared, as seen here,

"Prince Harry has devil-may-care attitude of Diana and Philip's blunderability"

"Then there was Oakland Raiders quarterback Ken Stabler, whose devil-may-care attitude made for deliciously naughty stories".

Daredevil

Although there is a Marvel Comics character named ***Daredevil***, in common usage the expression refers to a bold person who deliberately likes to take risk; sometimes recklessly. As in this headline,

"***Daredevil*** pilot is captured on camera flying the world's smallest twin-jet aircraft at 5,000 ft."

Making a Deal with the Devil

Making a deal or pact with the devil (also called a ***Faustian pact***) comes from the legend of Dr Faust, an intellectual alchemist who is said to have sold his soul to the devil's agent Mephistopheles in exchange for knowledge. But if you thought you could only ***sell your soul*** to the devil, you would be wrong.

Turns out over 7,500 people ***legally sold their soul*** to British retailer GameStation in 2010 when they failed to read the fine print during their online purchase. No harm no foul- it was an April Fool's Day prank by GameStation.

Of course, if you make a deal with the devil, you will also have to pay the devil for services rendered or rather have ***the devil to pay***, another way of saying that there will be serious trouble.

In the movie "Gettysburg", the Union Brigadier Buford tries to keep the Confederate soldiers off the high ground. Knowing that he is heavily outnumbered until reinforcements arrive, he says in a dialogue,

"There is the ***devil to pay***".

So how much is one's soul worth? Per Business InSider, - anywhere between a fiddle of gold for a half million dollars to a VSL (Value of a Statistical Life) for 8.5 million dollars.

Most folks, it seems are willing to settle for much less like a Roblox or a dutch oven. Here is one parent's account on the use of electronic babysitting during the pandemic,

*"My Kid Sold Her Soul to Roblox. I made a **deal with the devil** this summer. Lots of devils, if we're going to be accountants about it. But one in particular weighs heavy on my heart: Roblox."*

Another one from Food and Wine,

*"I Would **Sell My Soul** for This Dutch Oven. Does the devil take AmEx or just Bitcoin?"*

Children usually know how to push buttons and ***bring out the devil inside of their parents***, so keep those young minds busy because ***idle hands are the devil's workshop*** otherwise you will ***have the devil to pay.***

Devil's Advocate

As Inc.com explains it "One of the key roles that teams often get wrong is that of the **devil's advocate**. This is the person on the team who takes an opposing point of view and brings up contrary evidence and perspective. It's a key role to help make sure the team isn't missing a critical piece of information or failing to consider other options.

In 1587, the Catholic Church established the role of ***advocatus diaboli*** as part of the process of declaring someone a saint. The purpose of the role was to present counterevidence of sainthood and to find holes in the events presented as miracles. One of the most famous examples was when the atheist author Christopher Hitchens was asked to testify against Mother Teresa."

Usually in the canonization proceedings, there would also be someone with the role of **God's advocate**.

The **Devil's advocate** is also sometimes referred to as **The tenth man** rule. The essence is that if there are ten people in a room and nine of them agree on a course of action, then the tenth man should propose an alternate course of action to ensure all options have been considered. The term came into existence from the novel, "World War Z, 2006". By the way, did you know that an organization called the Satanic Temple is offering _Devil's Advocate scholarships_?

Here are some news headlines demonstrating use of the phrase,

"Guilty by Association: Why playing _devil's advocate_ on social issues is not helping anyone"

"Red Teams And _Devil's Advocates_: How To Make Use Of Contrarian Thinking"

"Stock splits: _playing devil's advocate_"

The Devil is in the Details

This might seem like a lot to wordplay but to understand the subtle nuances of culture, **the devil really is in the details**. This idiom means that even if something looks simple, the details are complicated and likely to cause problems when you get into the nitty-gritty. The phrase is also popularly used in the context of contracts or agreements. The earlier form of this idiom was **God is in the detail**. Here are some uses of it's expression,

"As always, _the devil is in the details_: the length of the fixed term, the range of variability and the behavior of the benchmark rate"

"_The devil is always in the details_, but most Americans are clearly on board with getting the pandemic under control and reviving the economy"

The Horn Effect

The horn effect (named for the horns of the devil) is seen used most often with the halo effect when discussing biases. Consumers can correlate a single negative experience with everything associated with a brand. This effect can also manifest itself during the hiring process in job interviews. As one interviewer quotes

*"There's a science behind what's happening here, known as the **halo effect and horn effect**, where we subconsciously allow one belief to overshadow others. I once hired an individual who had far less experience than the position required simply because they reminded me of myself when I first started my career. I subconsciously assumed they possessed the other qualities that I pride myself in, like integrity and accountability, only to find out later on that they lacked these characteristics. "*

Devil Food, Devil Sports and Devil Clothes

If you were not aware that **The Devil Wears Prada** is the name of a popular Hollywood movie from 2006, you may be mistaken into thinking that the devil was into luxury brands like Prada, Chanel, Givenchy, and Gucci. The movie is titled as such because the main character has a cold personality.

There are devil foods, although I am not quite sure if they are the devil's favorites. **Devil's food cake** is darker and richer than a regular chocolate cake and almost considered sinful and that is how it got its name. Boiled eggs seasoned with hot or spicy ingredients came to be known as **deviled eggs**.

And the Devil does not just figure in luxury clothing or hot or sinful food, but also in the name of a sports team. The Belgian national football (soccer in America) team is called *"**The Red Devils**"*. NHL-***New Jersey Devils***. And although one could go on about the Devil, the next topic in this category deals with Heaven, which makes for a much easier read.

Expressions with Religious Origins -Angels and Heaven

Angels

Angels are everywhere. Children are referred to as "*angelic*" and good Samaritans as "*angels in disguise*". A popular quote from the movie *It's A Wonderful Life* is

"*Every time a bell rings, an angel gets its wings*".

Angels are depicted as benevolent celestial intermediaries between God (or heaven) and humanity in Abrahamic religions (Judaism, Christianity, and Islam).

Therefore, ***Deals made in hell aren't witnessed by angels.*** It is a phrase commonly used in criminal law. The prosecution often must use witnesses which are not the most credible, sometimes they are even cooperating criminals.

This is the headline of an article on Michael Cohen, former campaign manager of the President,

*"Conspiracies Hatched in Hell <u>**Don't Have Angels as Witnesses**</u>"*.

But ***Fools rush in where angels fear to tread***. Sometimes shortened to ***Fools rush in,*** the phrase was first used over 300 years ago when 22-year-old Alexander Pope wrote <u>An Essay on Criticism</u>. It essentially means that a less experienced or informed person will sometimes rush into a situation where a more informed one would not.

An interesting use is in the title of this <u>Medium</u> article,

*"With COVID, Beware **When Fools Rush in Where Angels Fear to Tread"***.

Also, in this news headline

*"Only <u>**fools rush in**</u>: Beware of Valentine's Day scammers"*.

Guardian angels protect and guide. Seen as custodians, defenders and sometimes, even saviors, as in the following headline.

*"Barack Obama was Joe Biden's <u>**guardian angel**</u> at the Democratic debate"*.

Sometimes, citizens step up and protect their city when crime rates are high as in

*"<u>**Guardian Angels**</u> to patrol NYC in anticipation of election unrest"*.

Lucifer is not the only fallen angel. Per Investopedia, ***A fallen angel,*** in the investing world, is a bond that was initially given an investment-grade rating but has since been reduced to junk bond status. The downgrade is caused by a deterioration in the financial condition of the issuer.

The term is also sometimes used to describe a stock that has fallen precipitously from its all-time highs as in

"How Obscure <u>***Fallen Angel***</u> Penny Stocks Can Make You Rich"

"Potential *fallen angels* surpassed levels seen at depths of financial crisis, S&P says".

Entrepreneurs especially love angels who can make financial investments. Per Investopedia, an **angel investor** (also known as a private investor, seed investor or angel funder) is a high-net-worth individual who provides financial backing for small startups or entrepreneurs, typically in exchange for ownership equity in the company.

Angel investors: are they a bad idea for starting a small business? From Harvard Business Review

"Do Algorithms Make Better — and Fairer — Investments Than *Angel Investors*"?

The **halo effect** affects social perception of a brand. Per Wikipedia, a halo is "is a crown of light rays, circle or disk of light that surrounds a person". Angels have traditionally been represented with a halo and wings. The halo represents holiness.

The halo effect occurs when one positive experience with a brand, person or institute influences opinion positively in other areas or of other products from the same brand. As an article in Forbes is appropriately titled:

"Beware Of The Halo Effect: Choose Coaches For The Best ROI In The Digital New Normal"

Per this source, *"Popular culture often presents the idea that angels must earn their wings by successfully completing certain missions. One of the most famous portrayals of that idea occurs in the classic Christmas movie It's a Wonderful Life, in which a 'second class' angel in training named Clarence **earns his wings** after helping a suicidal man want to live again."*

The phrase is used on occasion to prove one's merit as the following examples demonstrate,

"After pair of losses, Silver Hawks *earn their wings* late by finishing strong for first win of season".

When used as follows on USA Network,

"An Angel *Gets Its Wings*! 'It's a Wonderful Life' ,

the phrase **Gets Its Wing** implies that a soul dies and becomes an angel, although this concept is disputed by many.

There are other anecdotal names with the word Angel. The popular American retail brand Victoria Secret's supermodels were known as "**Angels**". They would walk down the ramp during the annual fashion show with huge wings. **Angel Fish** is a species of shark with fins that appear like wings when spread horizontally. **Angel food cake** has a light and fluffy texture. Per Wikipedia, it earned its name because "it's so light that angels could eat it and still fly without being weighted down".

Popular legend states that an **angel of death** ushers' people from death to the afterlife. Josef Mengele was a Nazi doctor who came to be known as the **angel of death** during World War 2 due to his experiments on Jews in concentration camps which resulted in painful deaths.

Heaven

Although there are numerous definitions of heaven, the one that I like the best is from Dictionary.com "The abode of God, the angels, and the spirits of the righteous after death; the place or state of existence of the blessed after the mortal life".

I grew up accepting that the idiom "**To be in seventh heaven**" meant being in a state of blissfulness or happiness, but never really thought deeply about why it referred to the seventh heaven. Were there multiple different levels in heaven? Popular Hindu legends do talk about Swarga (Heaven) and a God named Indra ruling over it. On further research, I discovered that some Hindu religious books (Puranas) also describe seven levels of heaven. Abrahamic religions also have this concept, as did ancient Mesopotamians. It makes sense that the highest level would be the happiest one.

When Disney announced that its theme parks would be serving vegan food, the founder of a vegan dining guide wrote,

"Vegans and those seeking plant-based options are in <u>seventh heaven</u> with all the good news and awareness"

This news headline described Australia's cricket win against England in the multi-format women's Ashes as,

*"**Seventh heaven**: The day Perry destroyed England"*

To be "In ***Nirvana***" also has a similar meaning. The literal meaning of "Nirvana" in Sanskrit, is blowing out or quenching. Most associated with Buddhism, it is a state of freedom, from suffering and happiness. Nirvana is not a place; it is a blissful state of consciousness. Here are a few examples of its use in recent headlines.

"Alibaba Regulatory Woes A '<u>Nirvana</u> Set Up' For FAANG Stocks, Says Analyst"

The tech companies Facebook, Amazon, Apple, Netflix, Google are commonly referred to by the acronym FAANG.

"Top JPMorgan strategist explains how stocks hit market <u>nirvana</u> in 2021"

A similar idiom is "***To be on Cloud Nine***". The origin of this one is uncertain, but one theory is that Cloud nine refers to the Cumulonimbus cloud in a couple of weather classification systems. This thunderstorm cloud nine can rise above thirty thousand feet (6 miles) and would be quite close to heaven. However, the classification system has a total of ten clouds with the tenth number being the highest altitude one, so it does not make sense that the ninth one was chosen to be the happiest one. The upper altar of the Temple of Heaven, located in Beijing, China, is decorated with nine stones symbolizing the importance of the number nine in Chinese cosmology and the nine levels of heaven.

Cloud nine was also the name of a popular album released by George Harrison (Of the Beatles fame) in 1987. This news headline describes the mental state of football fans on hearing news about an offer made to a popular professional football player.

"Let the Games Begin: Some Manchester City Fans on *Cloud Nine* after seeing Harry Kane Update"

If my blog post went viral, I would also be on ***cloud nine***.

Another idiom that refers to the altitude of heaven is "***Stinks to high heaven***". The origin of this one is also not reliably known but it is used to either signal a very corrupt practice or a really bad smell. A similar phrase is used in Shakespeare's Hamlet where Hamlet's uncle says,

"*O, my offense is rank, it **smells to heaven**; It hath the primal eldest curse upon it, A brother's murder*".

Here are some examples of its usage,

"Russia's doping ban lifted: 'Frankly, it *stinks to high heaven*"

"*Lawyer says case against ex-Selma cops stinks to high heaven*".

Another way of conveying that you are ecstatic could be to say "I ***died and went to heaven***". This would be analogous to saying, "I'm ***floating on cloud nine***" or "I'm ***in the seventh heaven***". By the way, several food sites have a recipe for Died-and-Went-to-Heaven chocolate cake. A news headline screams,

"*I have **died and gone to heaven**: Domino's launches new chocolate orange cookies - and fans are already going wild for the gooey treat*".

Per Wikipedia, "***Pearly gates** is an informal name for the gateway to Heaven according to some Christian denominations. The twelve* *gates were twelve pearls, each gate being made from a single pearl*". The phrase is often used to denote that someone has died, as in these articles,

"They were holding hands when they left this world and went to the pearly gates"

"From a distance, the swaying leaves appear like happy children playing, while a closer view makes me wonder if this is what the wind chimes at the Pearly Gates look like".

A news heading references this as ,

"Dogs in Heaven? Pope Francis Leaves *Pearly Gates* Open".

A match made in heaven implies perfect compatibility. When the news of SalesForce acquiring Slack hit the media, Marc Benioff, the CEO of Salesforce, called it a *match made in heaven*.

Pennies from heaven denotes a windfall or unexpected money. As in this article that discusses the federal paycheck protection program,

"But for some, as grotesque as it seems, the pandemic has been a bonanza. Pennies from heaven. Except they weren't pennies. And the cash didn't come from heaven, but from taxpayers".

Music on earth has also been associated with heaven. ***Tears in Heaven***, about the death of his four-year-old son, was Eric Clapton's bestselling single song in the US. ***Stairway to Heaven*** , a classic rock song released in 1971 by the English Rock Band Led Zeppelin, has been voted on in several lists to be the most popular song ever.

Heaven forbid, you use some of these expressions in the wrong context. Which is why it is so necessary to understand them properly. And of course, I am willing to ***move heaven and earth*** to write posts that will get you to a complete understanding. ***For heaven's sake***, do read all my other posts in this category too.

Expressions with Religious Origins -God

God

This post discusses phrases that have the word "God" appear in them. Phrases related to God are embedded in our psyche. They are everywhere. We say, "Thank Goodness", "God Willing", "So help me, God", "Honest to God". O.M.G. is a popular emoticon. _God Bless Our Homeland Ghana_ is the national anthem of Ghana.

Per Wikisource,

**"God Save the Queen** is traditionally used as the national anthem of the United Kingdom and the royal anthem of Canada. It is one of two official national anthems of New Zealand. When the British monarch is male the anthem becomes **God Save the King"**.

Taking God's Name in Vain

"*<u>Taking the Lord's Name in Vain</u> May Seem Harmless to Many, but Not to All*", per this headline of an article in a popular Human Resources website. The religious underpinning of this is that the phrase occurs in one of the top ten commandments in Christianity, "Thou shalt not take the name of the Lord thy God in vain, for the Lord wilt not hold him guiltless that take his name in vain".

The phrase "***Taking the Lord's Name in Vain***" is in common use and is used to mean that God's name was taken in a way that is wrong or worthless. There are strong opinions on this, and a well-written perspective linked below is from the Seattle Times on the use of ***OMG***, which is ubiquitously used in chat rooms and text messages,

"*Oh my gosh! Should I say <u>OMG</u>?*"

Sections of society have tried, at times, to prevent taking God's name in vain. A classic book "Fahrenheit 451", on which a popular documentary was based, is taught in high schools across America. This book came under fire because of profanity and *<u>using God's name in vain</u>*.

An Italian soccer player was banned in 2020 for the same reason,

"*As Roma's Bryan Cristante has fallen victim to Italy's strict ban on <u>taking God's name in vain</u> on the pitch, picking up a one-match ban for blasphemy*"

An outdated law in the state of Indiana in the US attempts to outlaw using God's name in vain by children, as this news article goes on to describe,

"*An 1854 ordinance made it illegal for children under the age of 14 to swear, but only if that swearing is in some way <u>using God's name in vain</u>*"

Along with smoking cigarettes and playing cards, taking God's name in vain had some serious repercussions, per a CNN article that described life under ISIS rule in a town on the Turkish-Syrian border in 2015,

*"Taking **<u>God's name in vain</u>** could lead to prison; smoking cigarettes, a public lashing; playing cards, being locked in a cage for days"*

As God is my Witness

This is a phrase that some people use as an oath. There are contradicting opinions on it's use and it is sometimes considered as another example of taking God's name in vain. Nevertheless, it is used, not uncommonly.

Perhaps the most famous quote to use this phrase is from the classic novel 'Gone With the Wind' by Margaret Mitchell, and in the movie by the same name. Based on the American Civil War, the protagonist Scarlett O'Hara says the lines below when she returns home to find her plantation in ruins.

*"**<u>As God is my witness, as God is my witness</u>** they're not going to lick me. I'm going to live through this and when it's all over, I'll never be hungry again. No, nor any of my folk. If I have to lie, steal, cheat or kill. As God is my witness, I'll never be hungry again."*

Here is another example from an online article,

*"Maybe this pandemic has finally cracked open my sanity like a roasted chestnut. But **<u>as God is my witness</u>**, I spent the next hour doing dishes and cleaning countertops and tapping my toes and loving Christmas songs that used to make me gag "*

A popular use of the phrase has been,

"**<u>As God is my witness</u>**, I thought turkeys could fly."

This one comes from an episode of a TV show aired in 1978 when 20 live turkeys are tossed from a helicopter as part of a live radio broadcast and the radio station manager utters the lines above.

Act of God - Force Majeure

The name of God is also used in our legal contracts. Insurance, lenders, landlord-tenant contracts sometimes have a provision, specifically for an **Act of God**, in a Force Majeure (French for 'Supreme Force') clause. Generally, an *Act of God* applies to catastrophic events that occur naturally (E.g., Tornadoes, Earthquakes), whereas Force Majeure also includes events that occur from human intervention. In both cases, the events are outside the control of the affected party (E.g. War).

Whether the recent pandemic could be classified as an Act of God is not cut an dry, as this headline from a post on a popular online legal subscription services states,

"Coronavirus as an Act of God: Force Majeure Clauses Explained"

An article in Wall Street Journal is titled

"Some Acts of God are better than others"

The author goes on to write that a fallen tree is way better than water damage or a fire. Her article is also an excellent example of the use of another phrase that we will see in Part 4 "To get Religion". The article quotes *"You get religion real fast when you're standing in an apartment that looks like a burnt marshmallow. An elderly tenant lit his suite up with a cigar butt that he inadvertently left smoldering in an upholstered chair"*.

Alpha and Omega

Alpha and Omega is a phrase that designates the comprehensiveness of God, per Britannica. They are the first and last letters of the Greek alphabet and imply that God includes all that can be.

Here is a quote from a state legislator, emphasizing the importance of state legislatures,

"In my office in Washington, I use my chair from the Virginia House of Delegates that I bought when both chambers were renovated back

in 2008. It's old, and the springs are shot, but it reminds me that in our system of government, the states are the <u>alpha and omega</u>. It was the states that created the Federal government, and it was the states that created our local governments as well. Our founders set up a system of, by, and for the people that placed the state Legislatures at its very heart, and that heart still beats strongly today".

An article on the allure of sports trilogies has these lines,

"But, by far, <u>the alpha and omega</u> of sports trilogies remains Ali and Frazier. Kilroy is adamant: Nothing compares to those three bouts. "

Fit for the Gods

Although it is said that God eats and drink ambrosia and nectar, the phrase **fit for the gods** usually denotes something of high quality. It is often used in the context of food but has also been used to describe events and houses. The news headline below applies it to describe a digital music fest held in April 2020 during the pandemic lockdown:

"Technology blends with tradition to serve a digital music fest <u>fit for the Gods</u>"

Another example is in this article in the Washington post extolling the virtues of Ghee (a form of clarified butter):

"Ancient Sanskrit literature describes ghee as <u>fit for the gods</u>. Foods cooked in ghee are considered superior to those that eschew it"

Nectar of the Gods

There are several synonyms listed for the phrase ***Nectar of the gods*** to describe a drink such as aromatic, tangy, tasteful, edible, appetizing. In Greek mythology, <u>Nectar</u> was called the divine drink that the Olympian gods had.

In Hinduism it is called "Amrit" and there is a legendary story of the churning of the ocean between the Devas (Gods) and Asuras (demons) where the nectar of immortality rose out of the ocean.

Here is a headline that uses the phrase,

"Chateau Chantal's Ice Wine Festival to serve nectar of the gods"

And an article that discusses my favorite drink, coffee,

"Given coffee's popularity, it's surprising how much confusion surrounds how this hot, dark, nectar of the gods affects our biology".

Greek God

I have no idea why the phrase for a Greek Goddess isn't in popular use, but **Greek God** refers to a man who is handsome and well built, as the following examples demonstrate. An article on WWE (World Wrestling Entertainment) has the following lines,

"While not every single wrestler has the physique and the beauty of a Greek god chiseled out of granite, it certainly helps if you do".

Another headline describes a very popular Bollywood (The name for India's movie industry) movie actor:

"Behold the Greek God: Hrithik Roshan could make the sun melt with his hot looks"

God's country

Where does God live? **God's country** , per Wikipedia, is a name given to various **countries** and regions around the world, usually areas that are sparsely populated with wide expanses of nature.

"Not here in small-town America; we continued our legacy of kind hearts, friendly faces and caring for those that live with us in God's country"

*"This is a dirt road, a clay, dirt road way out in the middle of what we call **God's country**"*

The headline of an article that describes the Grand Staircase-Escalante National Monument in the state of Utah in USA is,

"When Everybody Wants A Piece Of *__God's Country__*"

The article has the following quote,

"We've always said it's **God's country**," Steed says. "The people from out here said that's because nobody'd have it but God, and now it seems like everybody wants it."

Godspeed

God speed is a way of wishing a person a safe and successful journey. Per this source, it was first used in Anglo-Saxon times 1,300 years ago. At the time, the phrase used was God Spoed You (speed was spelled as such in old English) and originally meant to signify prosperity and success. It also showed up in phrases "God spede me" and "God spede thee.

In 1962 when the famous American astronaut took off for the first US manned orbital flight, the backup astronaut for the mission, said the words,

"**Godspeed**, *John Glenn*".

When Bond Girl "Tanya Roberts" passed away, her former coworker said,

"We lost a great one. Rip #tanyaroberts you were a wonderful person to work with and we all loved you very much. *__Godspeed__*."

The Hand of God

The famous Argentine soccer (Football in many parts of the world) star , Maradona's 1986 World Cup Goal against England in the quarter finals will forever be imprinted with "*__The Hand of God__*". 25 at the time, the young Maradona appeared to the referee to have headed the ball against his taller opponent, but he had really hit the ball with the tip of his fist. England called for handball, but the goal was allowed to stand by the referee. Maradona claimed that the goal was scored " a little with the head of Maradona and a little with the *hand of God*". Maradona went on to score what is known as "the goal of the century" a few minutes after this goal in the same match.

The match happened four years after England claimed victory in the war over Falkland Islands against Argentina.

In the 2019 Asif Kapadia documentary about his life, <u>available on HBO Max</u>, Maradona showed no remorse for his nefarious goal.

"We, as Argentinians, didn't know what the military was up to [during the Falklands War]. They told us that we were winning the war. But in reality, England was winning 20–0. It was tough. The hype made it seem like we were going to play out another war. I knew it was my hand. It wasn't my plan but the action happened so fast that the linesman didn't see me putting my hand in. The referee looked at me and he said: 'Goal'. It was a nice feeling, like some sort of symbolic revenge against the English."

The phrase is still used on occasion, as the following news headline shows:

*"Messi tries to recreate **Hand of God** goal"*

This article uses it in the context of a defining moment for an English soccer play,

*"What are the defining Rooney moments? The big performances in finals? The reality-bending wonder-goals? What is Rooney's Istanbul 2005, his Villa Park 1999, his Euro 96, his **Hand of God**?"*

You can read more football metaphors in my blog post dedicated to them <u>here</u>.

God of Cricket

Sachin Tendulkar, a past cricket captain of the national team in India, is popularly referred to as the *"**God of Cricket**"* in India. A batting maestro who scored over a hundred centuries, he is frequently referred to as such in headlines and articles,

*"Will there ever be another **God of Cricket**?"*

*"Best And Memorable Innings By **God Of Cricket** Sachin Tendulkar"*

I also have a blog post dedicated to metaphors in cricket which you can read <u>here</u>.

God's Gift to Mankind

Devoted fans have sometimes described Maradona as a gift from God. Merriam-Webster defines ***God's gift to mankind*** as "used to describe the attitude of people who think that they are very talented, attractive etc."

A beautiful example of its usage from Satya Nadella, the current CEO of Microsoft , when he was talking about a day in the late '90s when Microsoft was the most valuable company in the world by market capitalization,

"People would walk around our campus thinking we are God's gift to mankind," relates Nadella. *"And, unfortunately, whether it's in ancient Greece or modern Silicon Valley, there's only one thing that has brought companies, societies, civilizations down, which is hubris."*

Another example is in this article exalting the virtues of Cabbage,

"Cabbage is a superhero among the category of leafy vegetables. You can add them to your diet by various means; be it boiled, cooked, steamed, sautéed, or even juiced. It has numerous medicinal properties, which could be credited as god's gift to mankind".

Godforsaken

The very opposite of God's gift to mankind is godforsaken. The literal meaning would be 'abandoned by God', but more commonly the phrase ***God forsaken*** is used to mean a place or something that is dismal, desolate, neglected.

An Op-Ed on refugees has the headline "*God's forsaken people*"

A state lawmaker had the following quote in a news article about militant activity in Kerala, a state in the southern part of India,

*"From **God's own country**, Kerala has transformed into God's forsaken country"*

Here are other examples,

"*We have something to lift our spirits after this <u>God-forsaken year</u> of 2020*"

"*As we close out this sprawling conversation, and as this <u>Godforsaken year</u> finally comes to a close, I wanted to take a second to acknowledge 2020's global box-office champion*"

"*I commuted into Vox Media's New York City headquarters for what would end up being the final time during the <u>godforsaken year</u> of 2020*"

Man Proposes, God Disposes

Per Wikipedia, "**The phrase Man proposes, but God disposes** is a translation of the Latin phrase "Homo proponit, sed Deus disponit" from a fifteenth century book by German cleric Thomas Kempis. It means that humans can plan all they want, but it would require God's will to make those plans successful. The news articles below show its common use,

"*<u>Man proposes, god disposes</u>. Having to cancel his India trip deprives Boris Johnson of the chance of sticking another feather in the cap of his Global Britain project*"

"*When the calendar date changed from 2019 to 2020 and the clock struck 12, we all looked forward to a year of traveling, being with friends and family, going to our normal work routine. But, as they say, <u>man proposes and God disposes</u>. All our 2020 plans were crushed by the coronavirus pandemic*"

"*The year 2020 kicked off with a lot of positive energy and hopes, a lot of set goals and major moves to better my life and family. But you know <u>man proposes, but God disposes</u>. He has the final say. The pandemic cut short a lot of dreams and aspirations. People died in thousands, jobs were lost in millions all over the world. In all I thank God for where I am today, I tried to recalibrate and navigate all the huddles caused by the effect of the pandemic*"

*"I now have learned that unlike what the poem Invictus says, we are not the master of our fate and the captain of our soul. Thomas Kempis said it rightly, **Man proposes and God disposes**. There we were with our strategic plans so organized in a Gantt chart and logical framework. But they were not meant to be"*

For context, Invictus is an English poem written in the Victorian times by William Henley. It has been used to inspire nations and people during times of crisis.

God Helps Those Who Help Themselves

A somewhat contradictory phrase to the one described above, this phrase was made popular by its inclusion in a 1736 edition of Benjamin Franklin's Poor Richard's Almanac.

Poor Richard was a character created by Benjamin Franklin in his writings and used in his yearly Almanac, which was published yearly for twenty-five years. The Almanac, like many others, featured monthly calendar events and lists. It also contained many proverbs, written with charm and expression.

The phrase continues to be in popular use, as evidenced by the following news articles,

*"The development of vaccines for COVID-19 in record time should reinvigorate our belief that those kinds of miraculous-seeming innovations are indeed possible — but they are far from certain. As the expression goes, **God helps those who help themselves**. If we want more of them, we'll need to turn away from a politics of complacency and resentment"*

An article from Sports Illustrated describes what it would take to get a surprise victory over another team in American football.

"As 7.5-point underdogs to the Pittsburgh Steelers, according to SportsBetting.com, if the Broncos are going to emerge from Heinz Field as the victors, they'll have to invert Murphy's Law and extract their best performances in those key moments. Perhaps they'll need a

little help from the Football Gods but regardless of one's beliefs; <u>*God helps those who help themselves*</u>*."*

God Works in Mysterious Ways

Humans can propose and hope that God will indeed help those that help themselves, yet sometimes they are lost feeling that God disposes in mysterious ways.

The proverb **God works in mysterious ways** comes from a hymn written by William Cowper in 1773, "God moves in a mysterious way."

Wiktionary describes this proverb as " *Expressing confidence that a conundrum has a solution despite it not being apparent or Commenting that a seemingly unfortunate or unfavorable situation or change may be beneficial later or in the long run*".

The headline of a heartwarming story,

"God works 'with mysterious people' as stolen items returned to church"

The article goes on to state "*We're pretty stoked at what God has worked through mysterious circumstances. We often say <u>God works in mysterious ways</u>, but he also works with mysterious people*".

Former American President Trump has also used the phrase at the presentation of the Presidential Medal of Freedom when describing his youth,

"But as we know, <u>God works in mysterious ways</u> . His wonders to perform — and in my first year of running, I became the national high school record holder".

Put the Fear of God into Someone

It is because of this uncertainty on the mysterious ways in which God operates, that the phrase **Put the fear of God into someone** is used to alarm or terrify someone, badly.

Some examples from news articles are,

"Experts in the estate planning industry estimate that the number of people drafting wills and trusts is also on the rise because of the pandemic, which has raised awareness and <u>put the fear of God in</u> people"

"Mike Flynn says he <u>put the fear of God into</u> Obama"

For context, Mike Flynn was a former national security advisor in America and former President Obama warned his successor not to hire him.

And in this excerpt from the book, "A twist of the knife", written by Peter James MacMillan, the feared becomes the fearer.

*"For 353 days a year – and 354 in a leap year – N.N. Kettering **put the fear of God into** restaurants around the world. On those dozen remaining days, something **put the fear of God into** him"*

And God said Let there be Light and there was Light

The shortened form of this phrase is used most often "***Let there be Light***". The full expression is originally in Hebrew and <u>found</u> in a book sacred to both Christianity and Judaism. The phrase is now humorously used in the context of illumination as the following articles show,

"<u>Let There Be Light</u>, and Art, in the Moynihan Train Hall"

"<u>Let there be light</u> At a glance, it looks like any other TV remote control from Samsung but the tech magic lies on the back of the clicker"

"<u>Let there be light</u> UNM researchers discover certain materials combined with UV light can kill coronavirus and other viruses"

"<u>Let there be light</u>: Take a drive around the Chicago suburbs to enjoy holiday displays"

Cleanliness is next to Godliness

Considered a old proverb and <u>popularized in a sermon</u> in 1978 by English preacher John Wesley, the phrase is primarily emphasize physical cleanliness, as the following examples show.

A quote from BBC travel story that describes how clean Japan is,

"In the West, we are taught that <u>cleanliness is next to godliness</u>. In Shinto, cleanliness is godliness"

A Wall Street Journal article that describes the history of cleanliness goes on to say,

"The saying <u>cleanliness is next to godliness</u>—credited to John Wesley, the founder of Methodism—was a great piece of free advertising, but it was soap's role in modern warfare that had a bigger impact on society. During the Crimean War in Europe and the Civil War in the U.S., high death tolls from unsanitary conditions led to new requirements that soldiers use soap every day"